UNSTOPPABLE
HOA BUSINESS
SUCCESS

THE ULTIMATE GUIDE ON BUILDING A RECESSION-PROOF
BUSINESS IN THE HOTTEST MARKET IN THE US WITH
VIRTUALLY NO STARTING CAPITAL

D1473860

JOAN MAGILL

JoanMagill.com

Testimonials

"Joan's book 'Unstoppable HOA Business Success' serves as an important reminder that those who have the ability to adapt and always rise to the occasion are never short of opportunities. She shares her experience and how she stays on top in an ever-changing industry."

Sharon Lechter, *Author, Speaker, Entrepreneur*

"Joan's charismatic personality is all you need, to whip up the perfect recipe for entrepreneurial success and then have the stickability to see through it."

Dr. Greg Reid, *Author, Speaker, Filmmaker*

"Joan's book aligns with my philosophy that 'Plan A is the only Plan B,' and her unwavering perseverance is a stellar example of how sticking to Plan A gives you all the success you need!"

Ron Klein, *grandfather of possibilities, Inventor of the Magnetic Strip on the Credit Card*

"Avoid what I refer to as BrandSlaughter and literally be the best in this rapidly growing national industry. Read 'Unstoppable Business Success' and learn specifically how. Clearly, there's no one better to share this golden wisdom than Joan Magill herself."

David Corbin, Author Four-time WSJ and USATODAY bestselling author, 'Mentor To Mentors', award-winning inventor, entrepreneur

"As someone who absolutely adores Joan, I think we can all learn something from her spunk and relentless tenacity!"

Nathan Minnehan, Author, Clothier, Publisher

JOAN MAGILL

JoanMagill.com

UNSTOPPABLE
HOA BUSINESS
SUCCESS

THE ULTIMATE GUIDE ON BUILDING A RECESSION-PROOF
BUSINESS IN THE HOTTEST MARKET IN THE US WITH
VIRTUALLY NO STARTING CAPITAL

Joan Magill

JoanMagill.com

ISBN: 9798378659913

Published by:

AUTHOR TO BE

www.authortobe.com

An imprint of:

Inspiration on Tap

www.inspirationontap.com

Inspiration On Tap

2336 SE Ocean Blvd #222

Stuart, FL 34996

SETTING THE BAR HIGH IN HOA/CONDO MANAGEMENT

As seen in FORBES, ENTREPRENEUR and Fortune 500 Magazine, the first woman to be on the cover of BUILDER Magazine and the founder of one of the longest-running condominium management companies

Joan Magill, founder of Residential Realty Group (RRG) is no stranger to the world of community management. She has been around the block for a while, quite literally! She has been around the houses, condos, high rises and every other property that she thinks has the potential of being 'managed.' With the knack for handling the fussiest finances, fixing up the most damaged houses and putting every building to the test, there is no challenge too big for this seasoned pro.

In her book, 'Unstoppable HOA Business Success,' she has unwrapped all the wisdom she has gained over time; doing landlord checks, running shopping reports and ultimately managing rentals. Her philosophy of staying nimble in an ever-changing market, facing every challenge with perseverance and discipline and always having a strategy in place, is reflected in every chapter of this publication. 'Unstoppable HOA Business Success' is just the roadmap you will need to become unstoppable in your journey to HOA business success!

Table of Contents

I. Foreward

By Nathan Minnehan

"Successful women understand that every day is an opportunity to learn, grow, and become better."

Sharon Lechter

Joan Magill is more than just a pioneer in the HOA business. She is an incredible leader with an indomitable resilience, and a true dynamo who is recognized for her spunky spirit and radiant energy. Her unwavering enthusiasm and a passion that never dies, has helped her forge a path of success and driven her to unparalleled greatness. Her energy is contagious, and she inspires others to be the best versions of themselves. Joan Magill, to say the least, is a force to be reckoned with!

One of the things that sets Joan apart is her remarkable adaptability. She understands that the HOA business is constantly changing, and she is always ready to adapt and evolve with the market. This positions her for success and always keeps her one step ahead of the curve. Not to forget her impeccable organizational skills. With a clear strategy for every aspect of her business, Joan is able to make quick decisions and seize opportunities at lightning speed, leaving the competition in the dust.

Luckily, Joan's adaptability and organizational skills are not limited to her work- they also drive her holistic approach toward life. She keeps an open mind toward opportunities for self-improvement and does not shy away from taking up new and complex challenges.

The winning combination of all of these unique traits is Joan's key to success, not only in the HOA industry but in every other aspect of life. As the market evolves and customer demands change, it's crucial to be able to pivot and change quickly in order to stay ahead of the game. A well-structured plan and a highly organized approach allow for efficient decision-making and the ability to capitalize on opportunities as they come your way.

Whether it's business or one's personal affairs, Joan's unique approach and exceptional leadership skills make her a true role model for all. Her captivating story and the invaluable insights shared in the book "Unstoppable HOA Business Success" make it a must-read for anyone looking to kick start or grow a business in the HOA industry or simply looking for guidance and inspiration in their personal and professional life.

II. Joan's HOA Journey

The remarkable story of a stolen family business, the Skip Snipper, and the art of staying nimble in an ever-changing market

'Get in the elevator, face everybody and smile.'

This is the mantra that Joan Magill grew up with and lived by for the most part of her life. She was fueled by this unwavering belief that every day was just another opportunity to light up someone's face with a smile. However, this positive spirit, this effervescence, wasn't born out of ease and comfort- it was forged out of grave hardships and some of the most transformational challenges that she could encounter.

As the founder of Residential Realty Group Inc.,one of the first and longest-running community property management companies established in Baltimore, Magill has proved to be a valuable asset for the board of directors of HOAs and condominiums, who look up to her for advice on key issues such as insurance, annual budgets, and property repair and maintenance.

Back in 1972, fresh out of the University of Maryland, Magill debuted her career in the real estate business by taking on the management of a rental development in Baltimore. To make ends meet, she was also teaching at a local middle school. At the same time, his father started a business that did landlord credit checks for tenants in Maryland. In no time, this family business was booming and his father had to hire someone outside the family to keep up with the expanding workload.

Tragically, the very person brought in to aid Magill's family in their prospering business ended up being the one who snatched it all away. He told the clients that the business was relocating, leading them to unwittingly flock to his strikingly similar new venture instead. Magill and her father were devastated. Just when they had lost all of their clients, Magill rushed to her father's rescue, joining the company full-time with the intention of selling it off.

"But in my head, I thought, how could somebody be so greedy and take such advantage of someone who is so generous? I just didn't understand the concept and I never will to this day."

It was this thought that moved Magill to the point where she decided she was going to get back all of her clients. She attended an expo where she bought and auctioned a dog at her booth and called him a Skip Snipper- the name that inspired the idea of skip-tracing. She started locating potential customers for real estate deals, all while cold calling her old clients, from her one-room office in her uncle's law firm and $250 in her accounts receivable. By December 1974, she got back all but one of her old clients.

While Magill had successfully re-established herself in the real estate industry, something was always missing. The bottom line was that she did not particularly enjoy what she was doing and was looking for better opportunities to challenge herself intellectually. She wanted to manage apartments because she loved every aspect of the work- the maintenance, the training, and even the marketing. The same year, she became active in the National Association of Home Builders (NAHB). At that time, she was the only woman on the Board of Directors for the Baltimore County Chapter and continued in this position for the next 8 years. She eventually rose through the ranks and was entrusted with the board's rental educational program.

Being the only woman on the Board, she found herself struggling with persistent discrimination, but she never let it come in the way of her progress.

"I found I was the only woman [on the board of the directors] at the time, and because I was young, nobody took me seriously," she says. "While I was incensed about it, I just made sure I was prepared at all my meetings and did my homework."

In a groundbreaking achievement, Magill was honored as the Associate of the Year from the Baltimore chapter of NAHB, becoming the very first woman to receive the prestigious award.

To further break into the industry, Magill started doing shopping reports on resident managers who worked in rental offices. To put it simply, she would pretend she wanted to rent an apartment and then report back to the landlord about the features of the property, and how she was treated throughout the process.

However, Magill's aptitude for constant learning meant that she did not just stop there.

She believed:

'If I don't know what to do, I will just learn it.'

Soon enough she was learning how to do landlord credit checks from her office managers. Her long-standing relationship with the real estate industry meant that she came in contact with the best developers, builders, and landlords. From budget estimations to property maintenance and the art of staying nimble in an ever-changing industry, she always got to learn something from them.

At the young age of 24, Magill decided that she wanted to manage rentals. At that time most rental apartments were handled by the buildings' owners, leaving little room for her to break in. However, just then, Magill stumbled upon a startling revelation - some developers had begun creating a new form of housing known as "private communities" or "condominiums." This innovative concept piqued her interest and set her on a course to explore this emerging trend in the real estate industry.

However, Magill was no ordinary real estate expert. Instead of just offering community management services to builders of condominiums, she sweetened the deal by volunteering to attend development and construction meetings. It meant that when the community units were being sold out, she could better educate future homeowners about the perks of the community lifestyle.

This was just the beginning of Magill's enduring success in the HOA/Condo management industry. By 1976, Magill started her first community management company. Today, more than 40 years later, the company, now called Residential Realty Group, is growing as strong as ever, empowering HOAs and condominiums with its top-quality services and guidance.

From the time Magill took the reins of her father's stolen business, to running a successful community management business, Magill has always been a force to be reckoned with! She has had the honor of being featured in FORBES, ENTREPRENEUR, and Fortune 500 Magazine and was the first woman to appear on the cover of BUILDER magazine. As one of the few first women in the real estate industry, she always wanted her work to inspire future generations.

Magill firmly believed in the idea of staying nimble, in an ever-evolving market, in the face of all adversities, and against all odds. With a positive, 'don-t stop- won't stop', go-getter attitude, she believed that anyone could accomplish anything. Through this book, she intends to share the wisdom and knowledge she has gathered over the years to help aspiring entrepreneurs make an epic breakthrough in the HOA/Condo management business.

Book Summary

"Success is not a destination, it's a journey. It's about becoming the best version of yourself."

Sharon Lechter

"Unstoppable HOA Business Success" is the ultimate guidebook for the most daring and ambitious entrepreneurs, who are on the path of conquering the HOA industry.

The purpose of this book is to provide guidance and inspiration to entrepreneurs who are looking to both jumpstart or expand their business in the homeowners association (HOA) industry. Written by the HOA mogul Joan Magill, who has thrived in one of the toughest markets in the United States, the book features her fascinating journey towards success. It is seasoned with wisdom that can help readers navigate the tricky waters of the HOA industry and build a successful, recession-proof business.

The book covers a wide range of topics, including how to identify and target the right market, build a strong brand and reputation, develop effective marketing and sales strategies, streamline operations and improve efficiency, build a loyal customer base, manage finances and cash flow, navigate the legal and regulatory landscape, and many more.

Unlike any ordinary publication this book is Joan's personal journal where she opens up about her entrepreneurial journey; sharing personal anecdotes and wisdom that she has garnered along the way. She candidly discusses the challenges she faced and the valuable lessons she learned at every turn, making the content relatable for anyone aspiring to launch or expand in the HOA industry.

But "Unstoppable HOA Business Success" isn't just for those in the HOA industry. Joan's strategies and tactics are versatile, applicable to any business, especially one that is surviving on limited resources. The book highlights the positive impact that a flexible and organized mindset has on one's business success, as well as personal progress.

To put it in a nutshell, "Unstoppable HOA Business Success" is an essential guide for anyone looking to break into the HOA industry and build a successful business from the ground up. Through Joan's expert advice and real-world case studies, readers will be equipped with all the right tools they need to navigate the complexities of the HOA industry, to develop powerful strategies and tactics, and to ultimately build a business that will stand the test of time.

Gear up to conquer the world of HOA!

Overview of the HOA/Condo Management Business

"Success is not a destination, it's a journey. It's about becoming the best version of yourself."

Sharon Lechter

The Homeowner's Association (HOA) or Condominium Management business is a rapidly growing industry in the United States, owing to the increasing demand for planned communities and gated neighborhoods. These companies play a vital role in keeping communities looking their best, from maintaining properties and common areas, to enforcing the community's rules and regulations. They perform a multitude of tasks, such as landscaping, snow removal, and enforcing rules on parking, noise, and other communal issues.

HOA and Condo management companies are typically

contracted by the community's board of directors, who are elected by the community's residents. They are responsible for the day-to-day operations of the community, including the management of finances, communication with residents, and coordination of maintenance and repair services. In short, they are the behind-the-curtain heroes, who are working tirelessly to make sure that the community continues to run like a well-oiled machine.

Just like any other business, HOA/Condo management companies also face a plethora of challenges on a daily basis. One of these is managing the expectations of the community's residents. Each community is unique, and the management company must be able to recognize and adapt to the specific needs of each community. This includes understanding the community's rules and regulations, being able to effectively communicate with its residents and having the ability to listen and respond to their needs.

Another important aspect of the HOA/Condo management business is financial management. The management company is responsible for regulating the community's annual budget and ensuring that all financial activities are in order. From collecting and depositing monthly assessments to paying bills, and preparing financial statements, these financial professionals ensure that their community's capital is well-organized. Moreover, when the time comes, the management company must also be able to furnish accurate and prompt financial information for the community's board of directors and residents.

Staying updated with the ever-evolving legal and regulatory landscape of the industry, is yet another challenge for HOA/Condo management. Laws and regulations vary from state to state, and the management company must have complete knowledge of the specific requirements of the state where the community is located. This includes understanding laws related to governance, meetings, and voting procedures, as well as laws related to finances, taxes, and insurance. Any legal conflicts that may arise, such as disputes between residents or between the community and outside parties, must be resolved by the HOA/Condo management.

HOA and Condo management companies are responsible for much more than just day-to-day operations. They also provide a range of additional services, including management of maintenance and repair projects, execution of events and activities, and implementation of community management software to streamline operations.

There is no doubt about the fact that the HOA and Condo management business is a challenging yet rewarding industry. It demands a special blend of leadership, effective communication, and the flexibility to understand and adapt to the unique needs of each community. However, beyond the effective and efficient provision of high-quality services, is the need for the management company to have friendly relationships with the community's residents and to build a positive rapport with the board of directors. To thrive in the HOA business, having a comprehensive understanding of the industry, along with its associated legal and regulatory requirements is the key. With all these attributes and qualities, the HOA/Condo management business becomes a fulfilling and exciting pursuit.

In conclusion, the HOA and Condo management business is a booming industry, brimming with opportunities for individuals that possess an entrepreneurial spirit. HOA management companies act as the pulse of the community; from physical maintenance to implementation of rules & regulations and financial management. Staying on top of one's game in the HOA industry can be tough but not impossible. It requires a clear understanding of the business, being fully aware of the do's and don'ts of the legal landscape and having a confident, communicative, adaptive and organized leadership style.

II. Three Compelling Reasons to Start a Recession Proof HOA/Condo Management Business

"Doing enough is never enough. Being enough is never enough. Success requires a higher level of action, drive and commitment."

Sharon Lechter

This chapter of "Unstoppable HOA Business Success," unleashes the potential of the HOA industry and convinces entrepreneurs why starting a recession-proof HOA/Condo management business is the right move. As the demand for HOA and Condo communities continues to climb, the prospects for business prosperity and financial growth in the HOA/Condo management industry become increasingly promising and tempting.

First on the list of reasons for starting an HOA/Condo management business, will be the explosive growth of HOA and Condo communities. Living in planned communities and gated neighborhoods has become trendy, which in turn has amplified the need for HOA and Condo management services. This opens up a unique window of opportunity for entrepreneurs to capitalize on this growing market and start a business that is in high demand.

Second, we will examine the premise of government support fueling HOA/Condo developments. With governmental agencies and municipalities jumping on board to promote the development of HOA and Condo communities, the demand for HOA and Condo management services continues to skyrocket. This governmental support provides a solid foundation for aspiring entrepreneurs to start their HOA/Condo management business, with ease and confidence.

Lastly, we will discuss one of the most attractive incentives for starting a HOA/Condo management business that is the industry's unfettered potential for professional growth and financial stability. Nothing sounds better than knowing that you have the opportunity of building a stable, profitable business with a consistent cash-flow profile and that is exactly what the HOA/Condo management industry offers entrepreneurs. This is primarily because it is a recession-proof industry that ensures financial stability even during the most tumultuous economic times.

The purpose of this chapter is to delve deeper into these three persuasive reasons and explore how they can benefit you as an entrepreneur. Additionally, we will also examine some of the most common and complex obstacles that you may encounter as a new business owner in the HOA/Condo management industry, and provide creative strategies for overcoming them in a sustainable manner. Whether you are a seasoned entrepreneur or are just starting out, this chapter will provide valuable insights and inspiration for starting your own recession-proof HOA/Condo management business.

Reason 1: Growth in HOA/ Condo communities

S tarting a HOA/Condo management business is an incredibly attractive opportunity and one of the biggest draws is the sustained growth in HOA and Condo communities. For the past several years the demand for planned communities and gated neighborhoods has been experiencing an upward surge and this trend of rapid growth is expected to continue in the future. In this context, the stats speak for themselves. According to the Homeowners Protection Bureau (HOPB), 67% of houses completed and 78% of houses built for sale, in 202, were part of a community association.

One of the main drivers of this growth is the democratic shift in the United States. The population is aging, and many retirees are looking for a low-maintenance, hassle-free lifestyle. HOA and Condo communities are offering just that- a sense of community and a wealth of amenities like swimming pools, tennis courts, and fitness centers. This has sparked an upsurge in the demand for HOA and Condo communities, which in turn has brought HOA and Condo management services to the forefront.

Increasing popularity of urbanization is another reason why HOA and Condo communities are growing at an alarming rate. As more and more people gravitate towards cities in a pursuit of upgrading their living standards, the demand for housing is increasing, accordingly. People are in a constant search for suitable alternatives that offer a comfortable and convenient lifestyle. Under these circumstances, HOA and Condo communities have emerged as an attractive option, offering a secure, tightly-knit community and a long list of features that are ordinarily not available in a single-family home.

The growth in HOA and Condo communities has also been driven by the recovering economy. As the economy rebounds from its recessionary slump, a larger number of people are financially empowered to fulfill their dream of homeownership. This increasing demand for new housing, including HOA and Condo communities has simultaneously made HOA and Condo management services the need of the hour.

Fortunately, the growth in HOA and Condo communities is a widespread national phenomenon, unfolding across cities, suburbs, and rural areas. This lack of geographical limitation gives enterprising individuals the opportunity to launch their HOA/Condo management business, anywhere and everywhere. Whether it is a bustling city, a tranquil suburb or an idyllic rural area, your dream business can now be exactly where you want.

In summary, the growth in HOA and Condo communities is the outcome of three key reasons; the changing demographic profile of the population, the accelerating process of urbanization and significant improvements in the economy. This growth has in turn created urgency in the HOA industry and an immediate need for HOA and Condo management services. Gated communities and planned neighborhoods have been drawing people in for several years now, and this trend is expected to continue in the future, posing a unique opportunity for new business owners to fill the gaping demand gap and capitalize on this rapidly growing market. The real icing on the cake is that the growth of HOA and Condo communities is not limited by geographical location, therefore providing a wealth of opportunities for those looking to get involved.

Reason 2: Governmental support for HOA/Condo developments

The recent attention given by governmental authorities to HOA/Condo developments is another plausible reason to tap into the industry. From funding to regulatory support and infrastructural implements; governmental organizations and municipalities are supporting and actively contributing towards the development of HOA and Condo communities. Governmental support adds credibility and stability to the development process and attracts a larger fraction of entrepreneurs who are looking to start a HOA/Condo management business.

One way that governmental agencies support HOA and Condo developments is through zoning laws and regulations. Many municipalities have zoning laws that allow for higher-density housing, such as HOA and Condo communities. By setting out clear standards for construction and design, these laws make it easier for developers to build HOA and Condo communities that have the visual appeal to attract both buyers and residents. They also enhance living standards by ensuring that HOA/Condo communities are meeting specific standards for safety, accessibility and environmental protection.

Funding is another productive way in which governmental agencies support HOA and Condo developments. Many municipalities offer financial incentives to developers in the form of tax breaks, low-interest loans, or grants. This financial boost makes it more economically viable for developers to build HOA and Condo communities. For instance, the FHA insured mortgage loan program has been making the process of purchasing and refinancing a home, risk-free and convenient, for years.

Governmental agencies also support HOA and Condo developments through infrastructure investments. Municipalities often invest in crucial infrastructure such as roads, public transportation, bridges, utilities systems and other public services that make communities more accessible and elevate the standard of human living. This not only attracts a larger pool of residents but also fuels demand for HOA and Condo management services.

Expanding on the premise of regulations, many governmental sectors have also implemented protocols that promote the use of HOA and Condo communities as a solution to housing affordability and availability. This is great news for low- and moderate-income households, turning their dream of homeownership into a tangible reality.

In summary, the government's role in the development of HOA/ Condo communities is both undeniable and equally valuable. Governmental authorities have been creating a positive and meaningful impact in the promotion of the HOA/Condo lifestyle through zoning laws, financial incentives, infrastructure investments, and other regulations. This governmental support provides a solid foundation for entrepreneurs looking to start a HOA/Condo management business, as it uplifts the demand for HOA and Condo management services.

Reason 3: Potential for business success and financial stability

As a recession-resistant industry, the HOA/Condo management business gives you the privilege of a steady income stream, even during economic downturns. Therefore, the third most compelling reason to start a HOA/Condo management business is the high potential for business success and financial stability. Even in the most unpredictable financial conditions, the HOA/Condo management industry provides entrepreneurs with the liberty to build a business that is financially stable and profitable.

There are several reasons as to why the HOA/Condo management industry has relatively higher financial security and protection. First and foremost are the recurring revenue streams. HOA and Condo management companies typically generate revenue from monthly or annual management fees, which provide a consistent stream of income. The steady cash flow brings a sense of security, predictability and reliability to the business, helping you steer through the fiercest economic storm, with confidence and ease.

Another reason for the financial viability of the HOA/Condo management business is the low start-up costs. By reducing the initial capital required to kick start the business, entrepreneurs can redirect their focus on building and growing it, instead of worrying about the costs associated with getting started. This makes the HOA/Condo management a more attractive option when compared to other types of businesses.

The HOA/Condo management industry is also characterized by a high level of stability, as the demand for its services does not fluctuate, compared to other types of property-related businesses, during economic uncertainty. This stability precipitates into entrepreneurial ventures, enabling them to maintain their success and economic consistency in financial conditions of all kinds.

Success in business does not always equate to the size of one's bank account. The internal satisfaction and sense of purpose that you attain from bringing a positive difference in others' lives is equally rewarding. As a service-oriented industry, the HOA/Condo management business is a great channel for those who yield satisfaction by helping others. As a management company, you intuitively become the backbone of the community; ensuring the happiness and comfort of its residents through your services. You will witness your efforts culminating in a positive change in people's lives, making it an incredibly fulfilling profession, while simultaneously motivating you to strive for greater success.

In summary, the potential for business success and financial stability is a compelling reason to start a HOA/Condo management business. From recurring revenue streams to low startup-costs and the inherent stability of the HOA/ Condo management industry, entrepreneurs are guaranteed a profitable business prospect. Additionally, as a service-based industry it provides the opportunity for personal satisfaction and fulfillment, something that goes hand-in-hand with financial gains, for business accomplishment.

III. Understanding the HOA/ Condo Management Industry

"Successful people are not necessarily the most talented; they're just the ones who never quit."

Greg Reid

Homeowners Associations (HOAs) and Condominium Associations (condos) are dynamic organizations that manage the common areas and shared amenities of a residential community. These associations are typically governed by a board of directors, composed of dedicated homeowners who volunteer their valuable time to manage the community, effectively and responsibly. The HOA/condo management industry is a crucial aspect of these organizations- managing their day-to-day operations, enforcing community rules and regulations, maintaining common areas, handling financial affairs and performing other administrative tasks.

One of the key responsibilities of HOA/condo management

companies is to maintain law and order within the community by enforcing community rules and regulations, outlined in the bylaws and covenants. These legal documents serve as the blueprint for organized community living and summarize important rules including parking regulations, pet restrictions, noise violations and limitations on rental policies. Moreover, they also dictate the rules governing common areas, like restrictions on their usage (e.g. pool hours, barbecues, etc). Other regulations include water disposal guidelines, storage of items in outdoor areas and maintenance of landscaping and exterior appearance. HOA/condo management companies are also responsible for enforcing architectural guidelines, which specify the types of improvements and modifications homeowners can make to their properties.

As mentioned previously, the maintenance of common areas falls under the jurisdiction of HOA/condo management companies. This includes landscaping, snow removal, and managing the community's amenities, such as swimming pools, tennis courts, and clubhouses to make sure that they are safe for the residents to use. Ultimately, the HOA/condo management companies hold the key to a well-maintained and secure community.

HOA/condo management companies are also entrusted with the financial affairs of the community. This includes collecting monthly assessments from homeowners, paying bills, and creating and managing the community's budget. HOA/condo management companies also work with the community's board of directors to create long-term financial plans for the community.

The HOA/condo management industry plays a crucial role in maintaining the standard of living and property values within residential communities. However, navigating the complex landscape of community management is not short of its challenges. One of the main challenges that HOA/condo management companies face is dealing with difficult homeowners. From those who disrespectfully flout community rules and regulations to those who find themselves in disputes with their neighbors, frequently, they require a nuanced approach to conflict management from HOA/condo management companies. These companies must step in as mediators and find a resolution that is both unbiased and preserves the rights of all parties involved, to ensure that the community remains a harmonious and equitable place for everyone.

Limited funds are yet another challenge for HOA/condo management companies. With a limited annual expenditure, these companies are compelled to make smart financial decisions to allocate resources effectively and efficiently. This requires meticulous prioritization of projects and expenses and the difficult task of determining which tasks need to be trimmed from the budget. At the end of the day, it is the duty of HOA/condo management companies to ensure that the community's capital resources are managed in the best possible way.

Navigating the complexities of the legal and regulatory terrain is yet another obstacle that HOA/condo management companies encounter. From staying up-to-date with the ever-changing state and local laws to ensuring compliance with federal laws such as the Fair Housing Act, HOA/condo management companies must have a deep understanding of the legal system that governs the HOA communities.

To ensure the highest quality of services, HOA/condo management companies should be staffed with a reliable team of well-trained and knowledgeable professionals. This includes managers, who should have experience in property management, as well as staff members who should be familiar with the legal and regulatory framework governing HOAs and condos. It's a bonus if the staff members are endorsed by professional associations such as the Community Association Institute (CAI) or the National Center for Condo, HOA, and Cooperative Association Studies (NCCHCAS), as certifications further underscore your expertise in the field.

To put it in a nutshell, the role of HOA/condo management companies is to keep residential communities running smoothly and enhance the quality of life for its residents. They are tasked with managing common areas, amenities, and financial affairs, while also tackling legal and regulatory requirements. Despite facing challenges such as difficult homeowners and budget constraints, these companies can overcome these hurdles by employing well-educated personnel, staying updated with regulations, and collaborating with the community's leadership (i.e. the board of directors). Ultimately, the aim of HOA/condo management companies is to provide superior management services that benefit the entire community.

Overview of the Industry

The role of the HOA/Condo Management industry in overseeing the daily functionalities of homeowners associations (HOAs) and condominium associations (condos) is undeniably crucial. They are responsible for a long list of managerial tasks, from enforcing community rules and regulations, to maintaining common areas and facilities, and administering the community's financial decisions.

To make things more complicated, the industry continues to face numerous challenges that are complex, time-consuming and demanding. Tackling non-compliant residents who refuse to abide by community rules and regulations, or mediating and resolving disputes between conflicting neighbors to reach a fair resolution, is just the tip of the iceberg. The Herculean task of budget management, with the availability of limited funds also rests on the shoulders of these companies. Under such circumstances, HOA/Condo management companies are required to prioritize spending and make difficult decisions about what can be cut from the budget.

Moreover, HOA/Condo management companies must have a thorough understanding of the legal and regulatory framework they operate in. This includes staying informed about the latest state and local laws that impact HOAs and condos, and ensuring compliance with federal laws like the Fair Housing Act. The Fair Housing Act prohibits discrimination in housing based on race, color, national origin, religion, sex, familial status, or disability. HOA/Condo management companies must ensure that they are not engaging in any discriminatory practices, and that their communities are in compliance with this federal law. Additionally, they must be knowledgeable about other federal, state, and local laws that may impact their operations, such as zoning laws, building codes, and property management regulations.

With an estimated 345,000 community associations in the United States and promising projections of continued growth, it is safe to predict that the HOA/condo management industry is highly competitive. In perspective of this increase in residential communities and the growing demand for HOA/Condo management services, the industry is poised for growth in the coming years.

In an industry characterized by intense competition, HOA/ Condo management companies must offer exceptional quality services to stay ahead. This means employing highly trained and knowledgeable professionals who possess expertise in property management and are well-versed in the laws and regulations that apply to HOAs and condos. To further demonstrate their commitment to providing top-notch services, these professionals should also hold certifications from reputable organizations such as the Community Association Institute (CAI) or the National Center for Condo, HOA, and Cooperative Association Studies (NCCHCAS).

To conclude, the HOA/Condo management industry has been instrumental in upholding property values and quality of life for residents in their communities. While the industry faces challenges such as dealing with difficult homeowners and limited budgets; hiring well-trained professionals, staying up-to-date with laws and regulations, and working closely with the community's board of directors, can ameliorate the situation. It is because these activities will enable HOA/Condo management companies can provide efficient and effective management services that benefit the entire community.

Different Types of Management Services

There are several different types of management services that HOA/Condo management companies offer to residential communities. The most common ones are enlisted and discussed as follows:

1. **Financial Management:** This includes collecting monthly assessments and fees from homeowners, paying bills, creating and managing the community's budget, handling reserve funds and working with the community's board of directors to create long-term financial plans. HOA/Condo management companies also maintain accurate financial records, and provide financial reporting and analysis, including budget forecasting and cash flow analysis. The goal of financial management is to ensure the community has a sustainable financial plan in

place and the funds are professionally managed.

2. **Administrative Management:** First and foremost, the administrative unit of an HOA/Condo management company is responsible for enforcing community rules and regulations, such as bylaws and covenants, as well as architectural guidelines for builders. Besides that, other administrative tasks include handling correspondences of letters, emails and other forms of communication, maintaining accurate records of all community transactions and activities, handling violations and coordinating meetings with the board of directors, community residents and other third-party stakeholders.

3. **Property Management:** This is a crucial component of HOA/Condo management as a secure, well-maintained property attracts potential buyers and residents. It includes the maintenance of common areas, such as landscaping, snow removal, regular inspections, repairs and activities that are necessary for the general

upkeep of the community's grounds and facilities. Property management also includes managing the community's amenities, such as swimming pools, tennis courts, and clubhouses, ensuring that they are properly maintained and safe for residents to use.

4. **Legal Management:** Compliance with local, state and federal laws is absolutely crucial for HOA/condo communities. Therefore, as part of their legal management services, HOA/condo management companies ensure that they are updated with the ever-changing state and local laws that pertain to HOAs and condos. In addition to that, HOA/condo management companies also take care of other aspects of the community's legal profile like providing legal advice to the community's board of directors, drafting and reviewing legal documents and representing the community in legal disputes.

5. **Insurance Management:** It is imperative that a community has adequate insurance protection against

potential risks and liabilities. In order to ensure this, HOA/condo management companies perform several different insurance management functions which include evaluating insurance needs, obtaining and maintaining insurance for the community, managing insurance claims and working closely with insurance brokers and providers to ensure that the community has the coverage it needs at the best possible price.

6. **Vendor Management:** From maintenance and repairs to event planning, vendors and contractors play a vital role in guaranteeing a high standard of living in an HOA/condo community. HOA/Condo management companies are entrusted with the task of managing these individuals and organizations. Their responsibilities include sustaining mutually beneficial relationships with vendors and contractors, negotiating contracts, managing payments & financial transactions and ensuring that vendors meet their obligations.

It's worth noting that some HOA/Condo management companies offer a full-service package that includes all of the above-mentioned services, while others specialize in specific areas, such as financial management or property management. Some smaller communities may opt for self-management and only require certain services such as legal and insurance management.

In conclusion, HOA/Condo management companies offer a wide range of services to residential communities, including financial management, administrative management, property management, legal management, insurance management, and vendor management. The type of services a community needs will depend on its size, complexity, and the specific needs of the community.

Key Players in the Industry

The foundation of the HOA/Condo management industry is composed of a variety of different professionals and property specialists. Some of the key players include management companies, individual managers, self-managed communities and industry associations and organizations.

1. **Management Companies:** These are professional companies that provide full-service management to residential communities. They typically employ a team of managers and staff who handle all aspects of community management. Their comprehensive range of services encompasses everything from financial management, administrative management, and property management to legal management, insurance management, and vendor management. Some examples of well-known management companies include FirstService Residential, Associa, and Cambridge Management Services.

2. **Individual Managers:** Contrary to management companies that are composed of a large number of employees, these are independent, self-employed, individuals who work on a contract basis with residential communities. They typically have a specialized skill set and may focus on specific areas of management, such as financial management or legal management. Due to limitations in size, scope and resources individual managers tend to have a smaller client base as compared to management companies.

3. **Self-Managed Communities:** These are residential communities who opt to manage and handle all aspects of community management on their own, instead of hiring a professional management company. These communities typically have a board of directors or a management committee made up of volunteer homeowners who handle the day-to-day operations of the community; from property maintenance, to financial management and even legal assistance. In

certain cases, these self-managed communities may choose to hire outside vendors or consultants for certain services such as legal or insurance management, but continue to retain overall control of the community. While self-managed communities allow its residents to enjoy a greater sense of control and autonomy, they achieve this at the cost of major challenges related to commitment, expertise in different areas of community management and time constraints.

4. **Industry Associations & Organizations:** It is noteworthy to mention the different industry associations and organizations that play a key role in the HOA/Condo management business. The Community Association Institute (CAI) is one of the most well-known organizations, providing education, resources, and networking opportunities for HOA/ Condo management professionals. Similarly, the National Association of Home Builders (NAHB) also provides resources to its members related to business management, housing advocacy and networking.

Every year, the association hosts the International Builders' Show (IBS), which is the largest annual light construction show in the world. The trade show attracts builders, remodelers, architects, designers and other professionals from the housing industry, making it the perfect platform for networking and gaining industry insights. Other industry organizations include the National Center for Condo, HOA, and Cooperative Association Studies (NCCHCAS) and the National Association of Residential Property Managers (NARPM).

In conclusion, the HOA/Condo management industry is composed of various important players including management companies, individual managers, and self-managed communities. Each of these players brings their own special touch and expertise to the table. Adding to the mix are industry organizations and associations who provide training, resources, and a platform for professionals to connect and grow in the industry. These groups help keep the HOA/Condo management industry on top of its game, ensuring residential communities receive the highest quality services.

IV. Starting your own HOA/ Condo Management Business

"Success is not a one-time event, it's a habit. It's something you do every day."

Greg Reid

Up until now we have learned that the rise of the HOA has engineered a rapidly expanding market for professional community engineers. Approximately 57,500 HOAs have community association managers while an estimated 8,500 HOA/condo management companies operate nationwide. This dynamic, highly-competitive profession has opened up a wide range of opportunities for entrepreneurs seeking to launch their own businesses. Venturing into the realm of HOA/Condo Management can be a challenging experience, yet equally rewarding and fulfilling. It requires a unique combination of business acumen, industry knowledge, and personal dedication.

This chapter is designed to act as a beginner's manual, giving you comprehensive guidelines on what it takes to start your own HOA/Condo management business. It will cover key topics such as identifying your target market, developing a business plan, obtaining the necessary certifications and licenses, and building a powerful team.

First things first, it's important to understand the target market for the HOA/Condo management services. This includes identifying the type of communities that would benefit from your services, and understanding their specific needs and challenges. It's also important to perform a detailed competitive analysis to help identify areas where your business can distinguish itself and stand out.

Once the target audience is framed, the next step is to prepare a well-crafted business plan, which will serve as a roadmap for success. A comprehensive business plan should encompass an overview of the business, a market analysis, a strategy for operations, a financial strategy, and a marketing strategy.

Acquiring the mandatory certifications and licenses is also an important milestone for starting a HOA/Condo management business. This includes obtaining a business permit and any other licenses required by your state or local government. In order to add more credibility to your portfolio and demonstrate your expertise in the industry, it is always wise to obtain professional certifications such as those offered by the Community Association Institute (CAI) or the National Center for Condo, HOA, and Cooperative Association Studies (NCCHCAS).

Finally, building a strong and competent team is indispensable for the success of any HOA/Condo management business. This includes recruiting experienced managers, as well as staff members who are familiar with the laws and regulations that pertain to HOAs and condos. Additionally, it is crucial to cultivate a network of trusted service providers and contractors who can supply the necessary support to the communities you oversee.

Starting your own HOA/Condo management business can be a challenging but rewarding endeavor. This chapter will provide you with all the necessary knowledge and tools that you will need to embark on this fulfilling journey towards a prosperous business.

Setting up the Business

"We can't solve everything we face… and we can't solve anything unless we face it!"

David Corbin

Like any other venture, setting up a HOA/Condo management business requires a combination of business savvy, extensive industry knowledge, and an unwavering commitment towards one's goals. The following steps outline the general process of setting up a HOA/Condo management business.

1. **Market Research:** Before launching a HOA/Condo management business, it's important to understand the target market for your services. Conduct a thorough analysis of the type of communities that would benefit from your services, such as their size, location, and demographic features. It is crucial for the success of your business, to understand who, where and why you are selling. In addition to this, it is important to have

an equally profound insight of one's competition. Identify your key competitors and your personal market strengths that you think can differentiate you from the former.

2. **Business Plan Development:** Any business would be lost without a well-crafted, robust business plan. It acts as a guide for streamlining and regulating operations so that you can reach your desired outcome without getting derailed. The business plan should include an executive summary, market analysis, operational plan, financial plan, and marketing plan. It should also outline your goals, target market, key competitors, financial projections, and strategies for growth and sustainability.

3. **Licenses and Certifications:** To prevent any legal distress, make sure you obtain all the necessary licenses and certifications required for operating in your state or municipality. This may include a business license, professional certifications, and specific certifications such as those offered by the Community Association

Institute (CAI) or the National Center for Condo, HOA, and Cooperative Association Studies (NCCHCAS).

4. **Team Building:** A dedicated and skilled team is the backbone of any business. Make sure that you invest in it wisely and generously. Build a workforce of proficient and knowledgeable professionals including managers with experience in property management and staff members who are familiar with the laws and regulations that govern HOAs and condos. Expand your network with vendors, suppliers and contractors who can assist you in provision of various services such as landscaping, repairs, pool maintenance, and security.

5. **Legal Structure Establishment:** Select a legal structure for your business that aligns with your objectives, personal & stakeholder liabilities, tax implications and ease of management, etc. It can be a sole proprietorship, partnership, limited liability company (LLC), or a corporation. Before the final decision, it's imperative to seek advice from legal and

financial experts to guarantee that all essential legal and financial paperwork is properly organized and compliant with applicable regulations.

6. **Acquire Insurance:** In case of any legal disputes or accidents, insurance can guarantee protection for your business and your personal assets. Collaborate with insurance brokers and providers who can help you acquire a suitable insurance policy that gives you the coverage you need at the best possible price. This can include liability insurance, property insurance, and directors and officers insurance.

7. **Marketing Plan Development:** Once you know what you are going to sell, it's time to strategize how you are going to sell it. Develop an innovative, customer-centric marketing plan that can effectively promote your HOA/Condo management business and attract new clients. If you have not already, then begin by identifying your target market, defining your unique selling points, and then developing a marketing strategy that will reach your target market. You can

use various marketing tools at your disposal such as online advertising, social media, or networking events.

8. **Start operations:** Once the aforementioned steps are completed, you are all set to embark on your HOA/Condo journey! It's time to ignite your entrepreneurial spirit and get started. This includes reaching out to potential clients, overseeing the daily operations of the communities you manage, and continuously evaluating your practices to improve your business processes.

In conclusion, undertaking a task as challenging as starting a HOA/Condo management business requires extensive research, strategic planning and an indomitable dedication to providing high-quality services to the communities you get in touch with. By following these steps and continuously striving for improvement, you can establish a successful and sustainable HOA/Condo management business.

Finding clients

Align with Builders as they are the best clients partners always creating new emerging HOA opportunities

L anding clients is a pivotal aspect of any HOA/ Condo management business. One tried-and-tested way to accomplish this is to align with builders, as they are often the best partners for creating new HOA opportunities. Here are a few marketing tools and tactics you can use to find and build strategic partnerships with builders.

1. **Networking:** If you are set out on a mission to find clients and align with builders, do not miss out on any networking opportunity. This includes attending industry events, joining professional associations, and reaching out to other HOA/Condo management professionals. Building relationships with builders and other industry professionals can lead to valuable referrals and potential clients.

2. **Leverage Social Media:** Social media has emerged as a powerful tool for exposure, advertising and relationship building. Create a professional profile on social media platforms and actively engage with other professionals and builders in your industry. Share insightful content and participate in online discussions to position yourself as a leading voice in the HOA/Condo management industry.

3. **Cold-Calling and Direct Mail:** While cold-calling and direct mail are relatively traditional methods of scouting for clients, they have not lost their efficacy over time. Make sure that your correspondence has a clear and compelling message that highlights your experience and expertise in the HOA/Condo management industry.

4. **Align with Builders:** Partnering with builders is a proven strategy for acquiring clients and generating new HOA prospects. Builders are constantly constructing new communities and developments,

making them ideal partners for creating new HOA opportunities. By joining forces with builders, you have the chance to provide your services to their newest communities and developments, laying the foundation for a long-lasting relationship.

5. **Offer additional services:** Attracting clients by offering them highly-demanding services as an add-on is another popular marketing strategy. Some of these services include energy management, asset management, and community engagement. Offering additional services, would automatically give you a strategic advantage over your competitors and position you for success.

6. **Build a strong online presence:** With a significant portion of the human population embracing the internet and its superpowers, building a strong online reputation can act as a magnet to attract new clients. This is predominantly because many potential clients perform online searches before choosing a HOA/

Condo management company. Make sure your website is professional, informative, and easy to navigate. Use search engine optimization (SEO) strategies to secure a top ranking in search results for relevant keywords. Additionally, make sure that your business is listed on prominent directories, such as Google My Business, and that you have a strong presence on review sites like Yelp and Angie's List. By putting your best digital foot forward, you're sure to make a memorable impression!

7. **Referral program:** Referral programs are an efficient and cost-effective method of bagging new clients. Incentivizing your current clients with discounts or gift cards, when they refer new business to you is an excellent way of leveraging the power of word-of-mouth and tapping into your existing pool of contacts. Besides expanding your customer base, referral programs also build trust and loyalty, as the referral comes through a reliable source.

8. **Build a reputation:** Widening your clientele requires you to position yourself in the target market as a reliable and trustworthy HOA/Condo management company. In order to gain this recognition, you must improve several different aspects of your business including the provision of high-quality, market-competitive services, engaging with existing clients and being responsive to their needs, exercising transparency in your communication and consistently delivering on your promises. By building a positive reputation, you can attract new clients through word-of-mouth and achieve long-term customer loyalty.

To put it in a nutshell, client hunting is a crucial aspect of any HOA/Condo management business and if done right, it can help you land clients that stay with you for a long period of time. A great way of finding clients is to align with builders as they might require your services on the new communities and developments they are working on. Networking, leveraging social media, cold-calling and direct mail, offering additional services, building a strong online presence, implementing a referral program, and cultivating a strong reputation are also effective ways to find new clients. By following these strategies, you can establish a strong client base and grow your HOA/Condo management business.

Building a Team

The foundation of every prosperous business is a team that is skilled, competent and committed to the growth of the company. Therefore, building the right team is crucial for the success of any HOA/Condo management business. Having a group of skilled and knowledgeable experts can guarantee that the communities under management are well-maintained and operate efficiently. Listed below are some key factors that you must bear in mind when building a team for your HOA/Condo management business.

1. **Experienced managers:** Experienced managers are a valuable asset for a HOA/Condo management business, as they bring a range of skills, knowledge and expertise that can be advantageous for the company in several different ways. When hiring, be on the lookout for managers with a proven track record in property management and a thorough understanding of the laws and regulations that affect HOAs and condos.

Shortlist managers with industry certifications such as those offered by the Community Association Institute (CAI) or the National Center for Condo, HOA, and Cooperative Association Studies (NCCHCAS) as they have demonstrated their expertise and commitment to the industry. Additionally, managers with experience in conflict resolution, budgeting, and financial management are highly sought after for HOA/Condo businesses. It's also important to look for individuals who have excellent communication and interpersonal skills, as they will be the primary point of contact for residents, board members, and other stakeholders.

2. **Staff familiar with rules and regulations:** The expertise and skills of staff members is as relevant as that of the managers. Shortlisting individuals who are familiar with the complex rules and regulations that pertain to HOAs and condos can be a real game-changer. Not only will they ensure that your business is legally complied, but will also serve as valuable allies for managers, offering them advice and support

in navigating the industry.

3. **Network of vendors and contractors:** When taking in account the external stakeholders of a HOA/condo management business, vendors and contractors land on top of the list. These individuals can provide a broad spectrum of services such as landscaping, pool maintenance, and security. Besides the physical maintenance of the properties under your management, vendors and contractors also play a significant role in helping you procure the best supplies for the development of the communities' amenities.

4. **Communication and collaboration:** Having clear and coherent communication, while simultaneously cultivating an inclusive culture are the key components of building a strong team force. Your company's corporate policy should emphasize honest communication among team members, and clearly define roles and responsibilities to ensure that everyone is aligned and on the same page. Poor communication

can have several consequences that are detrimental to the progress of the company, including misconceptions about work expectations, decreased efficiency and frequent conflicts between team members.

5. **Professional development and training:** Investing in the professional growth and skill development of your team members is crucial for building an efficient and dedicated workforce. Investing in training and development programs like online and in-person courses, workshops and seminars can help team members acquire new skills and knowledge, and to stay updated with the latest industry trends and practices.

6. **Employee retention:** Building a unified team, while employees walk in and out of the door, can be difficult. Replacing employees has a long-lasting reputational and cultural risk and can cost up to 400% of their salaries. This is why employee retention is such a crucial aspect of team building and the overall progress

of the company. To retain employees, it is important to provide them with a positive working environment, fair compensation, benefits and opportunities for growth and development.

7. **Lead by example:** The only way you can make your team members do something is if you do it yourself first. Leading by example is one of the most distinguishing features of a great leader determined to build an equally epic team. It is crucial for building a strong team. Demonstrate product work ethics like integrity, hard work, and a positive attitude. Show your team members that you are committed to the success of the company and that you are willing to work alongside them to achieve the company's common goals, as well as their personal growth aspirations.

Talking conclusively, hiring experienced managers and staff members who are familiar with the legal lingo, building a network of vendors and contractors, clear communication and a collaborative approach, opportunities for professional development and training, employee retention activities, and setting examples of excellent work principles are all the ingredients you need for successful team building.

Marketing and Branding

"You have to approach everything with a very positive attitude, there's nothing that can't be done. And age is not a barrier."

Ron Klein

Marketing in the present day is much more than just branding, locking leads, making sales, and growing your revenue. In today's digital age, it is the cornerstone of a winning management company. It can breathe life into many different aspects of your business. A well-targeted, data-driven marketing and branding strategy is bound to attract new clients and reinforce your position in the market as a reputable and trustworthy provider of HOA/Condo management services. The following are some key strategies to consider when developing a marketing and branding plan for your HOA/Condo management business.

1. **Identify your target market:** As important as it is to decide what you are going to sell, you cannot

achieve that successfully without knowing who you are going to sell it to. Identifying your target market is the first step in developing a marketing and branding strategy that hits the bull's eye. Take your time to understand the different types of communities and clients that would benefit from your services, and tailor your marketing efforts to specifically target these groups for higher chances of success. Evaluate these communities across various parameters, including demographic information, geographical location, lifestyle preferences, pain points and buying behavior.

2. **Develop a unique selling point:** The only way you can conquer the market is if your product does more than just sell- it stands out. Develop a unique selling point that sets your business apart from the competition. This could be a specific service offering, a unique approach to property management, or a commitment to exceptional customer service.

3. **Curate a selling online presence:** In this digital

era, there is a 100% chance that everyone is online; from your clients to contractors and competitors. Establishing a unique and powerful online presence plays an instrumental role in keeping you at the top of your game. This includes having a professional website, active social media profiles that carry industry-relevant content, and a strong presence on review sites like Yelp and Angie's List.

4. **Leverage content marketing:** Building a strong online profile also requires leveraging the power of content marketing. Craft insightful and engaging content, such as educational blog posts, visually appealing infographics, and informative videos, to draw in prospective clients and establish your business as a reliable authority in the HOA/condo management industry.

5. **Use email marketing:** Targeting a large number of potential customers, in an efficient, cost-friendly and measurable framework, requires a clever email-

marketing strategy. Create your targeted email listing, and make sure to include valuable content, such as industry updates, helpful tips and exclusive promotions in your email.

6. **Networking and events:** Attending relevant events and becoming a member of professional organizations can be a beneficial way to market your business and establish connections with potential clients. By participating in industry events, you have the opportunity to meet other professionals in your field and create valuable connections that can turn into new clients.

7. **Branding:** Effective branding can help build a strong reputation, foster customer loyalty, and ultimately drive business growth. A successful branding strategy involves creating a consistent and recognizable visual identity, including elements such as a logo and a consistent color palette.

8. **Referral programs:** Introducing a referral program that provides incentives to your existing clients for referring new clients to your business can be an effective way to acquire new customers and strengthen relationships with your current ones. By offering a reward, such as a discount or a special promotion, to clients who successfully refer new business to you, you incentivize them to actively promote your business to their own networks.

9. **Follow-up:** Marketing is an ongoing journey and staying in touch with potential clients is part of the process. Following up with your clients ensures that they are fully aware of your services and you are at their disposal to address any queries that you might have.

In conclusion, marketing and branding are critical components of a thriving HOA/Condo management business. To succeed, it's important to take a multi-faceted approach that incorporates a range of strategies, including identifying your target market, developing a unique selling point, establishing a strong online presence, leveraging content marketing, using email marketing, networking and attending events, branding, referral programs and follow-ups from potential clients. By incorporating these strategies into your marketing plan, you'll be well on your way to attracting new clients, building a reputable and trustworthy HOA/Condo management business, and securing your long-term success.

Financial Management and Forecasting

"Life's best rewards are not monetary in nature."

Don Green

A vital component of any HOA/Condo management company is financial management and forecasting. With a well-crafted financial strategy in place, you can ensure economic stability and make confident decisions for the future growth of your business. Here are some exciting techniques to keep in mind when constructing a financial management and forecasting plan for your HOA/Condo management enterprise.

1. **Create a budget:** Developing a comprehensive budget that outlines your projected revenue and expenses is one of the primary components of financial management. It will give you a clear picture of your financial circumstances and help identify areas where

you can cut costs or increase revenue.

2. **Keep accurate financial records:** No matter what business you are running, keeping an accurate, up-to-date record of your financial activities is an absolute no-brainer. This includes maintaining a detailed record of all transactions, including deposits, withdrawal and payments. These records provide a historical record of the financial health of your business, and can be used to monitor progress, identify trends, and make informed decisions.

3. **Use financial software:** Manually tracking and recording finances can be a time-consuming and tedious task. To ease this workload and gain valuable insights into your financial health, it is recommended to use specialized financial management software, such as QuickBooks or Xero. These software programs can automate many of the routine financial tasks, such as generating invoices, and provide valuable financial reports that can inform important business decisions.

4. **Monitor cash flow:** Monitor cash flow to ensure that your business has enough cash on hand to meet its obligations. This includes tracking your accounts payable and receivable, and monitoring your bank balances.

5. **Forecast future finances:** Forecast future financial trends by creating projections that outline your estimated revenue and expenses for the upcoming period. This proactive approach can help you identify potential financial challenges and to make informed decisions that position your business for success in future.

6. **Monitor and analyze financial metrics:** Monitor and analyze financial metrics, such as profit margins, return on investment (ROI), and net income. These metrics can help you to understand the financial health of your business and to identify areas where you can make improvements.

7. **Review financial statements regularly:** Review financial statements regularly to ensure that they are accurate and to detect any potential issues. This includes reviewing balance sheets, income statements, and cash flow statements. Regularly reviewing financial statements can help you identify trends and make adjustments to your business strategy.

8. **Seek professional advice:** Financial affairs can be tricky and complex. Therefore, do not hesitate from seeking professional advice from a financial advisor, accountant, or financial consultant. Their expertise can help you navigate the maze of financial management, with the ability to predict your financial future and highlight hidden risks and opportunities.

9. **Establish financial controls:** Establish financial controls to safeguard your assets, detect and prevent fraud, ensure compliance with financial regulations and promote the proper use of funds. This includes

creating financial policies and procedures and implementing internal controls such as segregation of duties, access controls, and regular audits.

To wrap it up, financial management and forecasting are the essence of any HOA/Condo management enterprise. By keeping a firm grip on these elements, you'll ensure the financial stability of your business, and make more financially viable decisions in the future. To hit these marks, consider implementing these essential strategies: craft a budget, keep meticulous financial records, harness the power of financial software, keep a close eye on cash flow, forecast future finances, analyze key financial metrics, regularly review financial statements, seek wise counsel from professionals, and establish rock-solid financial controls. By executing these strategies, you'll put your HOA/Condo management business on a strong financial foundation and set it on the path to success.

V. Strategies for Success

"Success is not about how much money you make, it's about the difference you make in people's lives."

Greg Reid

Starting and running a successful HOA/Condo management business requires a combination of clever planning, tenacity, and dedication. As the industry evolves and the market changes, it's essential to stay informed and adapt to new trends. In this chapter, we will explore key strategies for success in the HOA/Condo management industry, from navigating challenges, maintaining a competitive edge, recognizing growth prospects to crafting a strong reputation.

Challenges are an inevitable part of the entrepreneurial journey, and the HOA/Condo management industry is no exception. From natural disasters to difficult clients, having a strategic approach to tackle these hurdles and adjust accordingly is crucial for survival.

Competition in the HOA/Condo management industry is ruthless. In order to stay one step ahead of your competitors, it's crucial to stay informed about industry trends and best practices, in this ever-evolving market. Achieve market differentiation by offering unique services and solutions. The goal is to create a unique value proposition that sets a company apart from others in the market.

For any business seeking expansion and sustained success, recognizing opportunities for growth is a crucial step. By branching out into diverse realms or venturing into uncharted territories, you place your business on a path to prosperity and seize emerging opportunities as they come to light.

Brand image and reputation plays an instrumental role in building long-term relationships with customers, bagging new customers and giving the company a competitive advantage over its counterparts. In order to strengthen one's reputation, it's important to provide superior-quality services, engaging frequently and consistently with clients and maintaining open lines of communication. Additionally, building a strong online presence through a professional website, active social media profiles, and a presence on review sites like Yelp and Angie's List can also help establish your business as a reputable and trustworthy provider of HOA/Condo management services.

In this chapter, we will delve deeper into these strategies and provide practical tips and advice for implementing them in your HOA/Condo management business. Whether you're just starting out or looking to take your business to the next level, these strategies can help you navigate challenges, stay competitive, identify opportunities for growth, and build a strong reputation in the HOA/Condo management industry.

Navigating Challenges

There is no doubt about the fact that starting a business is an incredibly challenging endeavor and needs a winning combination of perseverance, hard work and dedication. An unimaginable number of challenges are thrown your way, from managing finances to tackling difficult clients, bearing the repercussions of unexpected natural disasters and much more. What is important is to always have a game plan in place to effectively address these challenges and adapt as needed.

One of the biggest challenges that HOA/Condo management businesses face is dealing with natural disasters. Unexpected events like hurricanes, tornadoes, and floods can cause significant damage to communities. Under such circumstances a disaster management plan is imperative. This includes identifying potential hazards, developing emergency protocols, and having a disaster recovery strategy in place. It's also important to have a plan in place to communicate with residents during a crisis and to provide them with information on how to stay safe. When facing a crisis, having a solid plan in place to communicate with those in your community and keep them informed on how to stay safe is paramount. It's crucial to ensure that residents are equipped with the knowledge they need to weather the storm and emerge unscathed.

Another common challenge that HOA/Condo management businesses face is dealing with difficult clients. This can include residents who are dissatisfied with the services provided, or quibble over costs and budgeting or homeowners who are difficult to work with. Having a plan in place to tackle conflicts head-on is a must. This means staying proactive with regular updates on the status of the community, being swift in addressing any raised concerns, and having an open ear to the needs of those you serve. In doing so, you can foster a sense of trust and stability, creating a thriving community where residents feel heard and supported.

A third challenge that HOA/Condo management businesses may face is to adapt with the changing market conditions. This can include a decrease in demand for HOA/Condo management services, or a change in regulations that affects the industry. As an HOA/condo management business, it's your duty to stay informed about any changes in the market and to be prepared to adapt and adjust as needed. This can include diversifying your services, expanding into new markets, or restructuring your business to meet the changing demands of the market.

In conclusion, the ability to navigate challenges is a vital component in the recipe for success in HOA/Condo management. Anticipating and planning for obstacles such as natural disasters, demanding clients, and market shifts is a must. With effective communication and a proactive approach, you'll be able to steer your HOA/Condo management business through even the toughest of storms and chart a course for long-term growth and success.

Staying Competitive

S taying ahead of the curve in any business is crucial, and the HOA/Condo management industry is no exception. While the market is in constant flux, it demands business owners to educate themselves about industry trends, developments and best practices. To set yourself apart from the pack, it is important to offer unique services and differentiated, tailored solutions.

One way to stay competitive is by staying current with industry trends and best practices. This includes researching your competition, identifying your target market, and understanding the needs and preferences of your clients. Additionally, regularly attending industry events and joining professional associations can help you stay informed about the latest developments in the industry and connect with other professionals.

Differentiation is key in staying ahead of the competition,

and offering unique services and customized solutions is a surefire way to do just that. Think outside the box and offer specialized services, like energy upgrades or cater to a specific niche, such as luxury properties. By going the extra mile and offering something truly unique, you'll be sure to capture the attention of potential clients and establish yourself as a leader in the HOA/Condo management business.

Maintaining exceptional customer service is a crucial aspect of success in the HOA/Condo management industry. From being responsive to clients' needs to providing prompt and dependable service, it's all about creating a positive customer experience and building brand loyalty. By establishing a reputation for delivering superior-quality services, you'll not only keep your current clients satisfied, but you'll also attract new ones.

Last but not least, having a robust online presence is a game changer in the HOA/Condo management industry. From showcasing your professional website to having an active social media presence and a strong reputation on review sites like Yelp and Angie's List, your online persona is an extension of your business. By building a strong digital character, you'll attract new clients, establish trust, and position your business as a leader in the HOA/Condo management world.

In conclusion, to thrive in the HOA/Condo management industry, it's all about staying ahead of the curve, offering a standout experience, and building trust with your clients. In order to achieve this, it's essential to stay in touch with industry trends and best practices, offer unique services, exceed your clients' expectations with exceptional services and solidify your digital presence as a leader in the market.

Identifying Opportunities for Growth

To secure long-term success, businesses in the HOA/ Condo management industry must stay attuned to growth opportunities that can arise at any moment. In this ever-evolving field, spotting opportunities for expansion is an important step in keeping ahead of the curve. Here are some innovative strategies for uncovering opportunities for growth in the world of HOA/Condo management.

1. **Diversifying your services:** A smart way to spot growth opportunities is by exploring new avenues and expanding your services. This can mean venturing into new areas such as property management or introducing fresh services. By branching out, you open up the possibility of reaching new audiences and boosting your revenue.

2. **Expanding into new markets:** Another way to tap into growth opportunities is by delving into new markets. This can include expanding your business to new geographic areas or targeting new client segments such as luxury properties or vacation rentals. By expanding your business into these new markets, you increase your chances of growing your customer base and elevating your revenue.

3. **Networking and attending industry events:** Networking and attending industry events can be a great way to identify new business opportunities and connect with potential clients. This can include attending trade exhibitions, joining professional associations, or participating in other networking events. By networking and attending industry events, you can stay informed about new developments in the industry and identify new opportunities for growth.

4. **Keeping an eye on the market:** Keeping an eye on the market and being aware of emerging trends can help

you identify opportunities for growth. For example, if you notice an increase in demand for energy-efficient upgrades or community development, you can explore ways to tap into these trends and grow your business.

5. **Leverage technology:** Technology is an ever-evolving field that presents a wealth of opportunities for growth. For instance, by utilizing property management technology such as software, you can streamline your operations, boost efficiency, and lower costs. By embracing technology, you can uncover new avenues for growth and enhance your overall performance.

In conclusion, to succeed and grow in the long term, it's crucial for HOA/Condo management businesses to be proactive in identifying opportunities for growth. By diversifying your services, exploring uncharted territories, building connections and staying informed,, and harnessing the power of progress through technology, you have the potential to uncover new growth prospects and set your business on the path to success.

Building a Strong Reputation

A stellar brand reputation will do half of the work for you if you are trying to run a successful HOA/Condo management business. It can help attract new buyers, retain current clients and increase revenue. Here are some strategies for building a strong reputation in the HOA/Condo management industry:

1. **Providing high-quality services:** Providing superior-quality services has the leading impact on building a strong reputation. However, it's important to understand that services extend beyond the premise of your product or your offering. It also includes being responsive to clients' needs, providing regular updates on the status of their communities, and addressing any issues or concerns promptly. By delivering outstanding services, you can cultivate a reputation for being a reliable and credible provider of HOA/Condo management services.

2. **Open communication:** Effective communication is key. Establishing and maintaining clear communication channels is crucial for constructing a robust reputation. This entails providing clients with timely updates on the condition of their communities, promptly addressing any concerns they might have, and educating them on how to remain safe during adverse situations. By ensuring open and transparent communication, you can foster trust and create a reputation as a responsive and dependable provider of HOA/Condo management services.

3. **Implementing digital marketing strategies:** Having a strong digital footprint has become a necessity in today's digital era. This includes having a well-designed website, engaging social media profiles, and a visible presence on popular review platforms like Yelp and Angie's List. By having a strong online presence, you can draw in new clients and establish your business as a credible and trustworthy provider

of HOA/Condo management services.

4. **Leveraging word-of-mouth marketing:** The most credible source of information is the genuine experience of people. This is why word-of-mouth marketing has become a highly effective tool for building a strong reputation in business. By fostering happy clients to leave positive reviews and leveraging their testimonials, you can cultivate trust and credibility for your business. Additionally, this type of marketing can help to spread awareness about your HOA/Condo management services and attract new clients who are searching for a reputable provider.}

5. **Being involved in the community:** Get involved in neighborhood happenings, offer your services for charitable causes, and take part in volunteer efforts. This not only showcases your company's responsibility and commitment, but also solidifies your reputation as an active and contributing member of the community.

6. **Providing exceptional customer service:** Providing

exceptional customer service is key to building a strong reputation. This includes going above and beyond to meet the needs of your clients, and making sure that their reservations are adequately addressed. By providing exceptional customer service, you can establish a reputation for being a caring and dedicated provider of HOA/Condo management services.

7. **Continuously Improving:** In a market that is continuously evolving, change is inevitable and every HOA/condo management business should embrace it confidently. Continuously improving and adapting to the changing market can help you build a strong reputation. Make sure that you are constantly updated with changing trends in the market and adapting your company's values and offerings accordingly.

In the end, establishing a credible reputation is a crucial ingredient for success in the HOA/Condo management industry. By consistently delivering top-notch services, staying connected with clients, showcasing your business online, harnessing the power of word-of-mouth, making a positive impact in your community, prioritizing customer satisfaction, and never resting on your achievements, you can secure your business's place as a trusted provider of HOA/ Condo management services, attract new clientele, foster loyalty among existing ones, and drive growth.

VI. Conclusion

"Success begins with imagination and is followed by belief and action."

Sharon Lechter

Starting any business is a remarkable feat and the HOA/Condo management industry is no exception. It requires skill, dedication and making the right move at the right time. In this comprehensive guide, we delve into the intricacies of this unique industry, providing you with valuable insights and actionable strategies for success. From tackling obstacles and staying ahead of the competition to unlocking growth opportunities and establishing a sterling reputation, this book covers it all. By exploring the critical components that make HOA/Condo management businesses successful, you'll gain a deeper understanding of how to turn your vision into a reality.

In this chapter, we will summarize the key takeaways and

provide recommendations for the steps ahead. We will also discuss some of the most common mistakes that businesses make and how to avoid them. By following the strategies outlined in this book, you will be well on your way to building a successful HOA/Condo management business.

It's important to remember that running a business is a continuous process, and as the market evolves, it's essential to stay informed and embrace new challenges. The strategies outlined in this book are not meant to be a one-size-fits-all solution, but rather act as a launching pad for your own unique business. By embracing change and continually seeking opportunities for enhancement, you'll secure the lasting prosperity and expansion of your HOA/Condo management venture.

In this chapter, we will also discuss the future of the industry, including emerging trends and technologies, and how they may impact your business. We will also provide resources and additional reading materials for those interested in learning more about the HOA/Condo management industry.

Finally, this book has served as a complete manual for making a successful debut in the HOA/Condo management industry. By adhering to the strategies presented here and accepting change and improvement, you'll set your business on a path towards long-term success and growth. This concluding chapter serves as a recap of the key takeaways and your next steps towards business greatness.

Summary of Key Takeaways

In this book, we have explored the various aspects of the HOA/Condo management industry and provided strategies for success. The key takeaways from this book are:

- Navigating challenges is a vital part of running a successful HOA/Condo management business. Having a solid strategy to tackle commonplace challenges, such as natural calamities, demanding clients, and market shifts, is the key to long-term success.

- Staying competitive in a high-demand market should always be on your radar. From industry trends to innovative practices, nothing should miss your eye. In order to stand out from the competition, make sure that your offerings are unique, differentiated and personalized. Besides that, focus on maintaining a high standard of customer service, and having a strong online presence. By remaining competitive, you'll not only attract new clients but also solidify your reputation as a reliable and trustworthy provider of top-notch HOA/Condo management services.

- Identifying opportunities for growth is essential for any business looking to expand and succeed in the long term. By diversifying your offerings, expanding into new markets, networking and attending industry events, keeping an eye on the market, and leveraging technology, you can identify new opportunities for growth and position your business for success.

- A strong reputation is imperative for success in the HOA/Condo management industry. By delivering high-quality services, fostering open communication, enhancing your online image, harnessing the potential of word-of-mouth, engaging in your community, delivering impeccable customer support services, and consistently improving, you'll not only establish your business as a trusted and respected provider of HOA/Condo management services but also attract new clients, retain existing ones, and drive revenue growth.

- It's important to remember that running a business is an ongoing process, and the market does not stop for anyone. The responsibility rests on the shoulders of each businessman to keep them updated with new innovations and breakthroughs in the market.

- Future trends in the industry, such as technology and sustainability, should also be considered and how they may impact the business.

- It's essential to stay informed and take advantage of the resources and additional reading materials available to learn more about the HOA/Condo management industry.

By following these key takeaways, you will be well on your way to building a successful HOA/Condo management business. Remember that success is not a one-time event, but rather a continuous process of learning, adapting and improving.

Future of Industry

The HOA/Condo management industry is dynamic-constantly evolving, to make space for more innovative practices and diversified services. Companies that are proactive and flexible are more likely to be positioned to succeed in the years to come. Here are some of the most significant trends that are likely to shape the future of the industry:

- Technology: Technology is playing an increasingly important role in the HOA/Condo management industry. From property management software to mobile applications, technology is being used to improve efficiency, reduce costs, and provide better services to clients. For example, property management software can automate tasks such as rent collection, maintenance requests, and financial reporting.

Mobile apps can allow residents to make payments, submit maintenance requests, and access community information from their smartphones.

- Sustainability: Sustainability is becoming an increasingly important issue in the HOA/Condo management industry. Many clients are looking for ways to reduce their environmental impact, and HOA/Condo management businesses are responding by offering services such as energy-efficient upgrades and community development. By incorporating sustainable practices into your business, you can attract environmentally conscious clients and reduce your own environmental impact.

- Remote management: With the rise of remote working and the ongoing pandemic, more HOA/Condo management businesses are offering remote management services. This includes online portals for residents to access community information and make payments, as well as virtual meetings and remote management services. By offering remote management services, you can attract clients who are looking for a more convenient and flexible way to manage their communities.

- Community development: As people continue to downsize and seek community-style living arrangements, community development is becoming an increasingly common phenomenon in HOA/Condo management. It encompasses community engagement, events, and community building activities. By offering community development services, you can attract clients who are looking for a more knit-together and connected community.

- Data analytics: With the advent of big data and advanced analytics, more HOA/Condo management businesses are using data to improve their services. This includes using data to identify trends, improve efficiency, and make more informed decisions. A data-driven approach can provide more accurate and actionable information to your clients and improve your overall services quality.

- Cybersecurity: As technology engulfs every aspect of our professional and personal life, cybersecurity has become a serious concern. Developments like data protection and smart home integration, are shaping the future of the industry and providing new opportunities for growth and innovation. By keeping an eye on these trends and incorporating them into your business, you can stay competitive and prepare your HOA/Condo management business for long-term prosperity. Remember to always be open to change and continuously look for ways to improve and adapt to new challenges.

In addition to these trends, the industry may also see a shift towards more community-based and resident-centered management services in the future. This includes a focus on community engagement, resident satisfaction, and quality of life. As technology continues to advance, it may also lead to more virtual and digital services, such as virtual tours, virtual meetings, and online portals for resident communication and management.

Another trend that may gain momentum in the future is the use of Artificial Intelligence and Machine Learning in HOA/Condo management. These technologies can help automate routine tasks, make better decisions based on data analytics, and improve overall efficiency. They can also help to optimize maintenance schedules, predict potential issues, and improve communication between residents, management, and boards.

As the HOA/Condo management industry continues to grow and evolve, it's possible that we'll see a trend of consolidation and mergers between companies. With increased competition, larger companies may see the acquisition of smaller ones as a means of expanding their reach, gaining access to new customers, and offering a wider range of services. This consolidation could reshape the industry in exciting new ways and provide opportunities for continued growth and success.

As the HOA/Condo management industry continues to

evolve, it's crucial for businesses to keep up with the latest developments and advancements. By embracing new trends, technologies, and strategies, you can give your business a competitive edge and ensure the sustainability of its prosperity. So, stay alert, stay informed, and be ready to take on the exciting changes that the future holds for the HOA/ Condo management industry.

Encouragement to Take Action

We understand that starting a business can be a daunting task, but it's important to remember that success does not happen overnight. It is a constant process of learning, adapting and improving to finally reach your destination. By taking the time to plan and implement the strategies outlined in this book, you can put yourself on the right path to success.

In order to succeed in the HOA/Condo management industry, it's important to stay in the know and stay ahead of the curve. Keep an eye on the latest industry happenings by attending events, connecting with peers, and staying on top of market trends. This way, you'll be able to spot new opportunities for growth and keep your business thriving in an ever-changing landscape.

It's also important to remember that building a strong reputation takes time and effort and one must not get impatient. It requires a multi-faceted strategy that encompasses, providing high-quality services, maintaining open and transparent communication, investing in building a strong digital profile, leveraging the potential of human experiences, participating in communal activities, providing exceptional customer service, and continuously improving.

It's also important to remember that starting a business requires a significant investment of time and resources. It's essential to have a solid business plan in place and to be prepared for the ups and downs of entrepreneurship. What makes the journey easier is having a team that can support you and help you achieve your goals. This may involve hiring employees, contractors, or consultants to help you with specific tasks. By building a strong team, you can ensure that your business runs smoothly and efficiently.

At the end of the day, don't forget that embarking on a HOA/ Condo management business venture is not a solo mission.

Surround yourself with a supportive network, be it a mentor, a business coach, or a community of entrepreneurial peers. Having this backing will not only provide valuable insight but also be a lifesaver in overcoming any obstacles that come with starting and running a business.

So, to wrap it up, running a successful HOA/Condo management business is a challenging but rewarding endeavor. By following the strategies outlined in this book, you can turn your dreams into a tangible reality. Remember to stay positive, stay focused and take positive action towards your goals.

About the Author

As seen in **FORBES, ENTREPRENEUR and FORTUNE 500 Magazine, the first woman to be on the cover of BUILDER Magazine and the founder of one of the longest-running condominium management companies- meet Joan Magill.**

Joan Glasser Magill, Founder of Realty Residential Group, Inc. is an extraordinary female entrepreneur who has achieved great success in both for-profit and nonprofit property-related organizations. Starting her property management business journey at the young age of 19, Joan is a visionary who has created and built niche businesses from scratch, filling voids in the market both regionally and nationally.

With a degree in education from the University of Maryland, College Park, Joan's career took an unexpected turn when she started a centralized credit check company for prospective renters. This innovative idea had never been done before, and it resulted in improving cash flow for landlords. Joan's leadership quickly earned the respect of her peers, despite facing difficult circumstances as the only woman on many professional association councils and boards of directors.

Today, Joan is a national consultant and expert witness in high-profile cases, as well as an active board member for several organizations. She is passionate about empowering and creating sustainable entrepreneurship opportunities for women and children, and promoting the best products and services.

Joan's impressive list of licenses and affiliations, including memberships in the Better Business Bureau, National Association of Realtors, and World Wide Association of Female Professionals, showcases her commitment to excellence in all areas of her professional life. She is also a managing partner at Feed Your Children Now!, Creative Money Works, Inc. & Creative Money Matters, LLC to help meet the needs of low-income, underprivileged children. Her ability to channel her generosity in her personal life is truly commendable.

JM

JOAN MAGILL

WWW.JOANMAGILL.COM

Made in United States
North Haven, CT
01 March 2023

33412461R00075